CYNTHIA UNGER

# An Introduction to the Universal Laws: A Magical Journey

"There is nothing going on around you that is more important than what is going on inside of you."

Cynthia

# Contents

# Preface

The Universal Laws came into my life gradually, unfolding like a series of hidden treasures. Life experience and an insatiable curiosity led me to explore their deeper meaning and profound impact. I stumbled upon these laws in my mid-20s, and as I reflect now, I don't recall ever encountering them earlier. Yet, when I began to study and apply them, it felt as though I had discovered a missing piece of life's puzzle—one that holds the power to make life flow with greater ease, harmony, and purpose.

At first, it was as though I had been left out of a great secret, one that reveals the beauty of how our thoughts, actions, and energy shape the world around us. I began to notice patterns: moments where life seemed to align perfectly with my intentions, times when embracing gratitude and positivity made challenges feel lighter, and the many ways my energy rippled outward, influencing others in ways I hadn't realized before.

This journey has been one of personal growth, awakening, and transformation. The Universal Laws are not just concepts to be understood—they are tools for living a more fulfilling, authentic, and abundant life. They teach us to embrace responsibility for our thoughts, to trust in the natural rhythms of life, and to create with intention.

It is my deepest desire to spark this same curiosity in you. To encourage you to look within and notice the ways these principles are already at work in your life. My hope is that this book serves as your invitation to begin—or deepen—your own journey of awareness. There is no right or wrong path, only the one that is uniquely yours.

As you read through these pages, my wish is for you to feel inspired, uplifted, and empowered. May the Universal Laws guide you toward a life that flows with ease and unfolds in the most magical ways.

With gratitude and love,

*Cynthia*

# Acknowledgments

*This book is the culmination of a journey inspired by many remark-able individuals, both well-known and deeply personal. To Napoleon Hill, Wayne Dyer, Bob Proctor, Abraham Hicks, and Rhonda Byrne— your teachings have been a guiding light, shaping my understanding of the Universal Laws and encouraging me to explore the profound connection between thought, energy, and the world around us. Your wisdom has left an indelible mark on my life, and this book is a reflection of the inspiration you've provided. To my family and personal friends—your love, encouragement, and unwavering support have been the foundation of my growth. You've inspired me to continuously strive to be a better person and have reminded me, time and time again, of the magic that comes from connection, kindness, and authenticity. This book is not just my journey—it's a tapestry woven from the lessons, support, and inspiration I've received from so many. I am endlessly grateful to everyone who has walked alongside me, offering words of encouragement, sharing moments of insight, or simply being present. Thank you for believing in me and for being part of this magical journey.*

# Introduction

An Introduction to the Universal Laws: A Magical Journey

The Universal Laws are the fundamental principles that govern life and the universe. They reveal the interconnection of all things and provide a road map for personal growth, fulfillment, and alignment with the natural flow of life. These laws aren't bound by time, culture, or belief—they simply *are*.

By understanding and aligning with these principles, we can co-create a life that feels authentic, meaningful, and abundant. The power of these laws is so magical that at times it can feel surreal—almost as if the universe itself is conspiring in your favor.

These laws have been studied and practiced by many throughout history, offering profound insights into how our thoughts, feelings, and actions shape our reality. The beauty of the Universal Laws lies not just in their wisdom, but in their simplicity: they are always at work, whether we're aware of them or not.

I invite you to remain open and join me on this journey. Together, let's explore how studying these laws and cultivating awareness of our thoughts, actions, and their ripple effects on the world can transform your life.

So, let's dive in! A world of magic, alignment, and limitless potential awaits.

# Chapter 1

The Law of Divine Oneness

Everything in the universe is deeply interconnected. Your thoughts, actions, and energy create ripples that influence the world in ways you may not always see. By embracing this connection, you can approach life with responsibility and gratitude, understanding that even the smallest actions hold significance.

**How to Apply the Law of Divine Oneness:**

1. Practice mindfulness and gratitude daily.
2. Take time to reflect on how your actions, thoughts, and energy influence the people and environment around you.
3. Commit to creating positive ripples—small, meaningful acts that contribute to the greater good.

*Gratitude and Connection: A Practical Exercise*

The Law of Divine Oneness teaches us that even the smallest actions can create ripples of positivity. Here's how you can embrace this principle in your daily life:

**Gratitude Reflection:**

Write down five things you're grateful for. They can be as broad as "the beauty of nature" or as specific as "the warm cup of tea I enjoyed this morning." Take your time to truly feel the gratitude as you write. I encourage you to use the space below to start your gratitude practice, but don't stop there. Make it a daily habit to reflect on the things you're grateful for. You might continue writing them in a notebook, revisit them in your mind as you lie in bed at night or before getting up in the morning, or even think about them during your daily commute. The opportunities are endless—find the moments that work best for you!

**Gratitude List:**

1. _____
2. _____
3. _____
4. _____
5. _____

**Bring Positivity into Every Room:**

- Before entering a room, take a deep breath and put on a genuine smile.
- Notice how this simple act changes how others interact with you.

**Random Acts of Kindness:**

- Smile at strangers throughout your day and silently wish them well.
- Observe how these small gestures can lift not only their mood but also your own.

**Practice Awareness:**

- Move quietly and attentively, simply noticing how your energy affects the environment and people around you.
- Pay attention to the subtle shifts in tone, energy, and connection.

By practicing these small yet profound acts, you're aligning with the Law of Divine Oneness—reminding yourself and others of the powerful interconnections we all share.

# Chapter 2

The Law of Vibration

Everything vibrates—your thoughts, emotions, and even your actions carry a frequency. High vibrations, like love and gratitude, attract positivity, while lower vibrations, like fear or anger, can create challenges. By consciously raising your vibration, you can shift your energy and influence your experiences in profound ways.

**<u>Reflect:</u>**

Have you ever entered a situation with anxiety and fear, only to watch it unfold just as poorly as you'd imagined? Now, think about what might happen if you approached the same situation with hope, confidence, and an expectation for a positive outcome. Could your mood and outlook change the result?

**<u>Try This:</u>**

The next time you face a situation with the potential for both good and poor outcomes, focus your energy on the good. Visualize the positive result you hope for, and notice how your mindset influences the reactions of those around you.

Remember, patience is key. The changes you experience may be subtle at first, but with continued practice, you'll begin to notice a shift—not only in how you feel but in how others respond to your energy. While you can't control every outcome, you *can* control how you show up, and over time, the effects will become undeniable.

### How to Apply the Law of Vibration:

Start your day with positive rituals that set the tone for a high vibration:

1. Listen to uplifting music.
2. Spend a few moments meditating.
3. Write down a few things you're grateful for.

Consistency matters. Commit to these practices daily, and allow yourself the grace to grow into this mindset. Subtle shifts often lead to the most profound transformations. Pay attention to how these practices influence your mood, interactions, and the flow of your day.

# Chapter 3

The Law of Correspondence

*"As above, so below; as within, so without."*

Your inner state reflects in your external world. When you cultivate inner peace, clarity, and balance, you'll notice harmony manifesting in your relationships, work, and environment. The closer your thoughts and actions align, the more smoothly life flows.

However, when you feel overwhelmed, it's important to pause and reassess. If you cannot change your actions to match your thoughts, consider shifting your perspective. Sometimes, the best path forward is to adjust your thoughts to accept your current actions.

**How to Apply the Law of Correspondence:**

**Ease the Pressure:** Tone down your demands. Ask yourself which change—your actions or your perspective—feels most comfortable and achievable right now.

1. **Cultivate Inner Peace:** Meditation is a powerful tool to reduce dissonance and bring clarity. It doesn't have to be elaborate—a simple practice of sitting quietly for 5 minutes or taking a few deep, intentional breaths can help calm your mind and reconnect you to your intentions.
2. **Observe Nature:** Use the balance and flow of nature as inspiration. Notice how it adapts seamlessly to change, and aim to bring that same adaptability and harmony into your daily life.
3. **Act with Intent:** Take a moment to ensure your actions reflect your true desires and values. Small, intentional adjustments can create big ripples of change in your external world.
4. **Reflect and Realign:** Be mindful of what feels most authentic to you. Whether you choose to adjust your actions or re frame your thoughts, prioritize the choice that brings you peace.

By practicing mindfulness and embracing flexibility, you can create a flow where both your inner and outer worlds feel more harmonious. Life isn't about perfection; it's about finding the balance that works for you.

# Chapter 4

The Law of Attraction

You attract what you focus on. Your thoughts, emotions, and beliefs act as magnets, drawing experiences that align with your energy. To attract what you desire, embody the energy of that outcome and take inspired action.

Take a moment to reflect—can you think of times in your life where the Law of Attraction has been at play? Perhaps it was a goal you were deeply focused on, a dream you couldn't stop imagining, or even a thought that unexpectedly turned into reality. This is my favorite of all the laws I've studied, and for good reason: it's transformative.

**<u>Watch Your Thoughts</u>:**

Pay attention to where your mind wanders. When your thoughts stray toward fear or doubt, gently bring them back to positive outcomes. Cultivate the habit of dreaming big and believing in the possibility of those dreams. The more power and focus you give to the Law of Attraction, the closer you'll come to seeing your dreams take shape.

**How to Apply the Law of Attraction:**

1. **Visualize:** Picture your goals as if they've already happened. Feel the gratitude, joy, and excitement of living that reality now.
2. **Align Your Actions:** Take inspired steps toward your dreams, no matter how small. Each action creates momentum and signals to the universe that you're ready to receive.
3. **Immerse Yourself:** Fit your dreams into your current reality as much as possible. If your dream is to live by the beach, visit often. While there, imagine what daily life would feel like—sink into those feelings until they become second nature.

The beauty of this law lies in its simplicity and power. By focusing your energy on what you want, aligning your thoughts and actions, and holding space for gratitude, you can co-create a life that reflects your highest intentions.

# Chapter 5

The Law of Inspired Action

While intention is powerful, action is necessary. Inspired action arises from intuition and alignment, guiding you effortlessly toward your goals. The key is to move with purpose, not pressure. Inspired action doesn't have to be grand or overwhelming—it often begins with small, intentional steps that build momentum over time.

**<u>Dreaming Is Action:</u>**

Dreaming is the first and most essential action. It helps you define your goals and align with the possibilities. As you continue to dream, add details that bring your vision to life. With clarity, small but meaningful actions will naturally present themselves.

**<u>Flow with Timing:</u>**

When you are fully in alignment, momentum builds at just the right pace. Trust that the universe will guide you and that the next steps will appear when the timing is perfect. Continual learning, whether through books, experiences, or conversations, will further open doors and opportunities you couldn't have imagined.

**How to Apply the Law of Inspired Action:**

1. **Listen to Your Intuition:** Pay attention to nudges and ideas that feel exciting or natural. They are often your next steps.
2. **Take Small, Intentional Steps:** Even the smallest action can move you closer to your dream. Don't underestimate the power of small but consistent progress.
3. **Trust and Adjust:** Be open to redefining your goals as you grow. Goals evolve as you gain new insights and experiences. Embrace this process and trust that it's all part of the journey.

By aligning with your intuition and taking inspired steps, you'll notice how effortlessly life begins to flow. The universe meets you halfway when you show up, ready and willing, for the adventure.

# Chapter 6

The Law of Perpetual Transmutation of Energy

Energy is always in motion, constantly transforming from one state to another. The beauty of this law is that you have the power to direct and shift energy—turning negativity into positivity through intention and action.

Be mindful of your thoughts and how your energy may influence those around you. Similarly, notice how the energy of others affects you. Nurture your energy by honoring healthy boundaries, but also be intentional about sharing positive energy. The ripple effect of even the smallest positive act can be extraordinary.

The more you practice this, the more natural it becomes to transform energy—turning frustration into gratitude, stress into calm, or even sadness into inspiration. It's an ongoing journey that deepens your connection to yourself and others.

**How to Apply the Law of Perpetual Transmutation of Energy:**

1. **Ground and Release:** Use grounding practices like walking in nature, meditating, or journaling to release negative energy and regain balance.
2. **Incorporate Rituals:** A mindful bath, complete with calming elements like Epsom salts or essential oils, can be a powerful way to reset and recharge.
3. **Quick Resets:** For a fast energy shift, try small intentional movements: stretch where you are, take a few deep breaths, or share a laugh or uplifting story with someone. Even a simple smile can transform your mood and brighten someone else's day.

Energy is contagious. By consciously choosing to transform and elevate your own energy, you contribute to a ripple effect of positivity that touches everyone around you.

### *The Ripple Effect:*

Every positive shift you make has the potential to inspire those around you. Whether it's your family, colleagues, or even a stranger passing by, your energy creates a ripple that touches others in ways you may never know. Like the gentle rise of sunlight filtering through the trees or the calming stillness of a morning pond, these moments of transformation remind us of nature's beauty—and our own ability to reflect that harmony in our lives.

# Chapter 7

The Law of Cause and Effect

Every action you take creates a ripple, setting into motion consequences that shape your life. This law serves as a reminder that nothing happens by chance—every result you experience stems from a choice, whether intentional or not.

It's not just about "positive" or "negative" actions but about being *aware* of the energy and intention behind your choices. When you act with alignment and purpose, you create outcomes that reflect your highest values. When you act unconsciously or from a place of fear or frustration, the consequences often mirror that disconnection.

The beauty of this law lies in its consistency. While you cannot always predict immediate results, trust that every choice contributes to your growth. Even perceived missteps offer opportunities for learning and refinement, guiding you closer to your desired outcomes.

**How to Apply the Law of Cause and Effect:**

1. **Pause and Reflect:** Before making decisions, take a moment to consider the potential ripple effects. Will this action align with the person you want to become or the life you want to create?
2. **Take Responsibility:** Acknowledge that you are the creator of your experiences. This isn't about self-blame but about empowering yourself to make conscious choices that align with your values and goals.
3. **Celebrate Small Wins:** Recognize that even small, intentional actions can lead to meaningful results. Whether it's a kind word, a thoughtful gesture, or a moment of gratitude, these choices create a chain reaction of positivity.
4. **Learn from Challenges:** Not all actions yield immediate or favorable results, but every outcome carries a lesson. Use challenges as opportunities to refine your choices and grow in self-awareness.

*A Different Perspective*

Think of the Law of Cause and Effect as a continuous dance between intention and outcome. Each step you take shapes the rhythm of your life. While you may not always control the tempo, you always have the power to adjust your next step.

# Chapter 8

The Law of Compensation

The energy and effort you put into the world will always find their way back to you, balancing the universal scales. This law assures us that what we give—whether time, energy, kindness, or resources—returns to us, often in unexpected ways.

**Balance the Scale:**

If you feel you haven't been as kind, generous, or outgoing in the past, know that it's never too late to start. Life is about balance, like a scale. Begin tipping the scale toward positivity with small, intentional actions. It doesn't need to be extravagant—start where you are.

**Simple Acts of Kindness:**

- Leave a larger tip than usual at a restaurant.
- Offer a smile to a stranger.
- Drop a dollar into the red kettle.

- Give someone a heartfelt compliment.

These small acts, when done consistently, add up and create powerful ripples of positivity. As you continue to give, you'll notice the scale tipping in your favor, bringing balance and abundance into your life.

### How to Apply the Law of Compensation

- **Start Small:** Kindness doesn't require grand gestures. Take small steps to create positive change in your environment and let the momentum build.
- **Be Consistent:** Keep adding to the scale of positivity with each thoughtful action. Over time, these small acts accumulate and transform both your life and the lives of others.
- **Trust the Process:** Even if you don't see the results right away, trust that the universe is keeping track. Focus on the joy of giving and let karma take care of the rest.

### *A Gentle Reminder*

Balancing the scale isn't about perfection; it's about progress. By consistently choosing kindness and positivity, you align with the flow of abundance and create a life rich in meaningful connections and opportunities. Tip the scale—one small act at a time—and watch how the universe responds.

# Chapter 9

The Law of Relativity

Challenges are not fixed—they are relative to how we perceive them. A shift in mindset can turn obstacles into opportunities for growth, and responsibilities into privileges. By changing how we view our experiences, we open the door to gratitude and resilience.

**Change Your Perspective:**

What if you re framed your daily tasks and challenges? Instead of thinking, *I have to*, try shifting to *I get to.*

- *I get to go to work and contribute.*
- *I get to drive the carpool this week and spend time with the kids.*
- *I get to wash the laundry and care for my family.*

This shift may seem small, but it has the power to create profound changes in how you approach responsibilities. Even unwelcome outcomes can teach us valuable lessons:

- *I got to participate.*
- *I learned from my trials and grew stronger as a result.*

By re-framing your experiences, you transform difficulties into opportunities for reflection, growth, and gratitude.

**How to Apply the Law of Relativity**

1. **Re frame Challenges:** When faced with difficulties, ask yourself, *What can I learn from this?* or *How can this help me grow?* Look for the silver lining in every situation.
2. **Practice Gratitude:** Apply the *I get to* mindset to your daily responsibilities. Notice how this small shift in language changes your attitude and energy.
3. **Celebrate Growth:** Recognize that even the most difficult challenges offer lessons that shape you into a stronger, more resilient person.

*A Gentle Reminder*

Life's challenges often come with hidden gifts. The Law of Relativity reminds us that how we view our experiences determines how we move through them. By shifting your perspective, you can turn even the toughest trials into stepping stones toward success and fulfillment.

# Chapter 10

The Law of Polarity

Life is a balance of opposites. Joy and sorrow, light and dark, abundance and lack—each is essential to the other, creating the full spectrum of human experience. This law reminds us that growth comes not from avoiding challenges, but from embracing both sides of life with gratitude and understanding.

**Finding Meaning in Opposites:**

*Life's contrasts often hold profound lessons.*

*Death brings grief*, but it also reveals the depth of love and cherished memories. To feel sorrow is to know the value of a loved one's presence and the gratitude for the time you had together.

*Watching children grow* is bittersweet. As they transition into new stages of life, you celebrate their growth and independence, yet you may long for the little ones they once were. These moments remind us to appreciate each phase of life fully, knowing they are fleeting.

### *Watching Growth and Embracing Change*

Growth, however, isn't just about the external changes we see in others—it's also about the internal evolution we experience within ourselves. As you continue to grow, you may find yourself saying goodbye to friends whose paths no longer align with yours or even letting go of pieces of yourself that no longer serve you well. While these changes can bring sorrow or uncertainty, they also create space—space for new experiences, connections, and opportunities for growth.

Saying goodbye isn't an end; it's an opening for transformation. By releasing what no longer fits, you make room for the people, ideas, and opportunities that will help you become the best version of yourself.

By accepting both joy and sorrow as natural cycles, we cultivate resilience and a deeper appreciation for life's journey.

### How to Apply the Law of Polarity

1. **Acknowledge the Cycle:** When facing difficult times, remind yourself that they are temporary. They are part of a larger cycle that will eventually bring clarity, peace, or even joy.
2. **Find the Lesson:** Reflect on what each experience—whether joyful or challenging—has to teach you. Life is full of lessons, and by observing and learning, you can

navigate future cycles with greater ease.

3. **Hold Both Gratitude and Grief:** Recognize that gratitude often accompanies sorrow. To feel loss is to have experienced love and connection. Embrace both feelings as part of life's richness.

### *A Gentle Reminder*

The Law of Polarity teaches us that no experience exists in isolation. The darkness helps us appreciate the light, and challenges strengthen our gratitude for moments of ease. By finding balance and meaning in life's opposites, we can navigate the cycles of life with grace and wisdom.

Growth often requires letting go, but each farewell holds the potential for new beginnings. Trust in the process and embrace the bittersweet beauty of life's transitions. With each phase, you are stepping into a more authentic and fulfilled version of yourself.

# Chapter 11

The Law of Rhythm

Life flows in natural cycles, from the changing seasons to the rise and fall of emotions, energy, and circumstances. By honoring these rhythms, we align ourselves with the natural ease and flow of life, reducing resistance and fostering balance.

**Honoring Your Own Rhythm:**

Just as nature moves through cycles of growth, harvest, and rest, so do we. Being mindful of how you're feeling—physically, emotionally, and mentally—and respecting your unique needs is essential for finding balance. Embracing what feels right for you, without concern for whether others understand, is a powerful act of self-care and self-respect.

It's important to recognize that not every phase of life will demand the same energy. Some periods may call for strength and high productivity, while others invite patience, reflection, or rest. By tuning into your body's signals and honoring where you are in the moment, you cultivate a deeper connection to yourself and the rhythms of life.

**How to Apply the Law of Rhythm:**

1. **Listen to Your Body:** Pay attention to how you feel. If you're in a slower phase, allow yourself to rest without guilt. If you feel a surge of energy, use it to take action and move toward your goals.
2. **Trust the Timing:** Not every season is meant for harvest. Trust that slower periods are essential for growth, just as rest is vital for renewal.
3. **Respect Your Individual Needs:** Let go of the need to explain or justify your pace to others. What matters is finding and honoring the rhythm that works for you.
4. **Embrace the Cycles:** Recognize that life's rhythm is always in motion. Embrace each phase—whether it calls for strength, patience, high energy, or rest—and know that it's all part of the greater flow.

*A Gentle Reminder*

The Law of Rhythm reminds us that life is a dance, moving between moments of action and reflection. By aligning with these natural cycles, we create space for balance, growth, and renewal. Trust your unique rhythm, honor your needs, and move with the flow of life.

# Chapter 12

## The Law of Gender

The Law of Gender reminds us that within every individual exists a balance of masculine and feminine energies. These energies are not tied to gender identity but represent complementary forces within all of us: the masculine embodies action, structure, and logic, while the feminine represents intuition, creativity, and flow. Achieving harmony between these energies allows us to experience fulfillment, balance, and authenticity.

### Finding Your Inner Balance:

At times, you may feel called to lean into your masculine energy—to take decisive action, plan strategically, or persevere with strength. In other moments, the feminine energy may guide you—to rest, nurture your inner world, or approach life with creativity and openness. Recognizing when each energy is needed, and honoring both as equal parts of yourself, is key to living in alignment.

## Honoring Your Needs:

Life naturally ebbs and flows between these energies. There will be times when fostering creativity feels right—when ideas flow effortlessly, and you're called to dream, imagine, and create. Other times will require resilience, focus, and the ability to execute with strength and determination. The balance comes in trusting your instincts and allowing yourself to honor what you need in the moment.

## How to Apply the Law of Gender

1. **Reflect on Balance:** Take time to assess areas of your life that may feel out of sync. Are you taking action but neglecting reflection? Or are you spending too much time in planning and intuition without stepping forward? Strive for balance.
2. **Embrace Action and Rest:** Recognize that both action and rest are vital. Just as seeds need time to grow after being planted, you also need periods of rest to recharge after taking action.
3. **Foster Creativity and Strength:** When inspiration strikes, allow your feminine energy to guide you—whether it's through art, problem-solving, or intuitive decision-making. When challenges arise, tap into your masculine energy to move forward with determination and focus.
4. **Create Space for Both:** Set aside intentional time for activities that nurture both energies. For example: _Masculine Energy_: Goal setting, structured planning, or strength-building exercises. _Feminine Energy_: Meditation, jour-

naling, or creative projects that flow naturally.

### A Gentle Reminder

The Law of Gender teaches us that balance is not about perfection but about harmony. By honoring both the masculine and feminine energies within you, you create a life that feels whole and aligned. Trust in the dance between action and intuition, creativity and strength, and know that each has its place in your unique journey.

# Conclusion

By studying and embracing the universal laws, you open the door to seeing your life unfold in the beautiful way it was always meant to. These principles act as a guide, helping you align with the flow of the universe and uncover the magic within and around you.

This guide is just the beginning—a stepping stone to introduce you to these profound truths. I encourage you to dive deeper, reflect on their application in your life, and explore where your own magical journey leads.

Remember, we rise by lifting others. As you grow, share your light with those around you. Together, we can create ripples of positivity and abundance that extend far beyond ourselves. It is my wish that we all soar—toward fulfillment, joy, and the highest version of who we are meant to be.

# Epilogue

*"There is nothing going on around you that is more important than what is going on inside of you."*
— *Cynthia*

Remember, as you navigate your journey through life, there is nothing going on around you that is more important than what is going on inside of you. Stay connected, stay present, and trust in your inner magic. Keep dreaming, keep believing, keep creating ripples of positivity and love. Let your life unfold in the beautiful way it's meant to.

With gratitude,

**Cynthia**

www.ingramcontent.com/pod-product-compliance
Lightning Source LLC
Chambersburg PA
CBHW031240120626
46545CB00003B/1208